How to Day Trade

A Complete Guide to Make Money Online, Trading on How to Day Trade

BY JOHN PARROT

© 2016

TABLE OF CONTENTS

INTRODUCTION

Day trading is an exciting, fast-paced investment practice that involves high risk and, when done correctly, high rewards. However, traders who take up day trading, and wish to be successful, will need to master certain skills that include being able to select the right stocks, follow risk management techniques, identify proper entries, and stick to a tested strategy. This book will provide you with guidance and techniques that will aid you in succeeding as a day trader.

Day trading is unique because you will be trying to make a profit in a short window of time with higher risk trades. There are a few practices that you should keep in mind throughout this book. Intraday returns, for example, are of greater importance to a day trader than annual returns because positions are only held for very short periods of time. Trading on margin is a tactic often employed by day traders to make big gains, but this is a very risky practice that could potentially ruin your day trading career. You will also engage in selling short, a practice that involves selling borrowed shares at a high price so you can buy them back at a lower price and make a profit. Buying to the long side will ensure that your maximum loss will be no more than the amount of shares you purchased. The market is long-biased and some stocks aren't available for shorting, so being a long-biased trader is recommended.

Understanding the concepts is important, but they alone will not make you a successful day trader. This book will discuss the fundamental concepts of day training as well as techniques essential for positive trade performance. To begin with, you will learn how to manage risk and predict volatility. You will learn how to make educated risks and when you should make them. This text will also identify why emotions can be detrimental to successful trades. Building your self-discipline and setting a stop loss is a good way to ensure your career as a day trader will have longevity and success.

CHAPTER 1: HOW FEAR CAN LEAD TO FAILURE

Day trading is a complex profession composed of daily risks that manifest themselves as losses or wins. As a result, statistics show that only 1 in every 10 professionals pursuing a career in day trading will be able to earn enough to sustain a living due to the challenges associated with consistently turning a profit.

No matter how much experience you have as a trader, it is impossible to devise a strategy that will guarantee success on every trade. However, by following the advice outlined in this chapter and avoiding some of the mistakes that often cause traders to fail, you will find that it is possible to achieve a successful, lucrative career in in day trading. In particular, you will learn why is important to understand and follow the rules of risk management and recognize how they can positively or negatively impact your success as a trading professional.

While the goal is to make an overall profit, it is important to become accustomed and prepared for losing. Failure to accept the risks associated making trading decisions or allowing emotions to guide your decisions could prevent you from achieving success in your career as a day trader. This chapter will help you identify and understand behaviors that day traders often fail to recognize as hindrances to their success.

Reality Check

The Holy Grail syndrome is often used to describe the behavior of traders who attempt to find a supposedly foolproof strategy to guarantee winning trades. The reality is that there is no automated trading system, perfect plan or indicator that can deliver a day trader 100% success. Fear of experiencing a loss causes many day traders to waste valuable time, money, and energy searching for this "Holy Grail," believing that their percentage of success is of more significance than their profit loss ratios.

The importance of profit loss ratios can be easy to miss. But for students to succeed as day traders, they should learn how to trade with a 2:1 profit loss ratio and understand why trading with negative profit loss ratios will result in failure. For example, a 2:1 profit loss ratio allows for profit with only a 50% success rate; meanwhile, a 1:2 profit loss ratio would only produce a profit if the trader was consistently able to achieve a 75% success rate. Therefore, it is considerably easier to make a profit following the 1:2 profit loss ratio.

Emotional Conditioning

Risk is a fundamental part of day trading, but it's important not to let emotions cloud your judgment when making decisions as a trader. Managing emotions can be tricky when attempting to navigate the market and anticipate trends, particularly in day trading. For example, fear might influence a day trader to react to quickly to rising or falling stocks. These quick decisions often do not give us the results we expected and can even end in a massive loss.

For example, emotional urges can lead you to sell a winning investment too soon because you fear it's reached its maximum value and will begin to lose. Although you've secured a profit by selling a winner, you've capped it before its full potential could be realized. Alternatively, fear can also cause you to hang on to a losing investment because you are afraid to take the loss; this often is the case for novice traders who believe they can salvage a losing stock given enough time. A successful trader knows to be patient with winners and to cap their losses.

Keeping Your Cool

Maintaining control of your emotions will allow you to look at your investments objectively and be realistic about their potential. Set rules for yourself, like the ones discussed above, to help you navigate winners and losers. Otherwise, you could end up losing money despite maintaining a high success rate. Loss, like profits, is part of the trading business and it's important to embrace them as part of the road to success. Remember that good day traders are also capable of being good losers because they know how to cap their losses and run their winners with discipline.

Discipline can help break patterns that are often adopted by novice traders who only learn from textbooks. While skills, practices, and concepts that come from a typical textbook are essential to your grasp of day trading, it is equally important that you've learned the significance of understanding and controlling your emotional response to the stresses associated with risk management.

Begin by acknowledging how your mindset is impacting your thinking or your approach to trading; self-awareness is a critical part of success. Journaling some of the emotions that come up while you are trading is a good way to keep yourself in check. Next, incorporate activities that require discipline into your daily routine. Regularly practicing discipline will make it easier to work through emotional urges and keep to the risk management rules you set for yourself as a trader.

Meditation, for example, is a useful activity for practicing discipline and reducing the stress that leads us to act on emotional impulses. As we discussed earlier, stress and fear can present a significant barrier to your success as a day trader. Practicing discipline can help you control the ways fear and stress causes urges and snap decisions regarding winners and losers. Physical exercise is another conditioning technique that can be used to train your brain to persevere through discomfort. It is important that you practice these techniques regularly so that you become accustomed to avoiding and overcoming emotional patterns that are negatively impacting your performance as a trader.

When combined with the knowledge and concepts you will learn from textbooks and experience, these lessons about keeping yourself cool, clear, and collected will help you find greater success in day trading.

CHAPTER 2: MANAGING RISKS

This chapter will familiarize you with how to pursue volume and manage risk as a day trader. Day trading, as opposed to long-term investing, is often sought because it presents the opportunity to make larger profits in a shorter amount of time. However, day trading also comes with greater risk than long-term investment techniques. Therefore, it is crucial that you understand the unique facets of day trading before embarking on your career.

For example, day traders can only efficiently utilize high-speed trading techniques with accounts between $25,000 and $1 million; the liquidity of the market cannot support the execution of multi-million dollar positions quickly enough. Still, diversifying your portfolio with long-term investments is a good technique for maintaining the success of your portfolio once your account becomes too large to efficiently day trade.

Because of the high-risk/high-reward nature of day trading, it is important to consider strategies that can maximize profit and minimize risk carefully. The previous chapter discussed strategies to help eliminate emotions that cloud judgment and hinder our ability to evaluate trade opportunities and the risks they pose with clarity. This chapter will identify several common types of risks that you will encounter as a day trader.

What Are You Willing To Risk?

To begin with, the price at which you are willing to sell for a loss should never be over your maximum dollar loss amount, and such decisions should always be based upon up to date support or a resistance area on the chart. Furthermore, although volatility presents positive and negative situations for all traders, day traders should note that it can complicate how we plan for losses and profits. For example, it is dangerous to day trade when the market is volatile because stocks can vary so widely under those circumstances; waiting for the market to stabilize is the best strategy for day traders.

Note that using leverage gives day traders an increased amount of exposure risk. Your exposure risk can be determined by multiplying the number of held shares by the price of each share. It is important to watch your level of risk and take steps to alleviate that risk, such as keeping your shareholdings short-term.

Stock halts are another type of event that can be difficult to predict and can be particularly problematic for day traders that use large positions. They occur at a market-wide scale as a result of technical glitches or circumstances caused by volatility. A halt can mean that your stock will close at one price and reopen at a much lower price, sometimes even below your maximum loss amount.

Circuit breaker halts, on the other hand, are put in place to help slow down the market when a stock rises or falls more than 10% in a 5-minute span of time. This kind of halt typically occurs when a company is planning to make a significant announcement. When the stock reopens, there is the risk that its value will have dramatically decreased as a result of the news.

It is important that day traders avoid stocks that are at high risk for stock halts. For example, penny stocks often undergo halts pending government investigation that can last several weeks or months. Furthermore, trading on margin is particularly risky when you consider the possibility of stock halts—don't put yourself in a position where you could potentially receive a margin call from your broker.

Keeping Track

Details of all your trades should always be tracked so you can review them later. Include information such as setup, symbol, time, price, entry and exit, the amount made and lost, and general notes. This will make it easier to evaluate trades that went wrong and possible areas for improvement. Keeping track of this information will also help you refine your trading plan and fill in any gaps that may have been contributing to losses. For example, beginner traders often fail to consider a max loss before entering a position.

When one particular trade results in a large loss, consider what your risk was when you entered the trade. Did you make a trade while in an emotional state that clouded your judgment? Were you afraid to take the loss? It is vital as a day trader you learn to take a loss when the price of a stock falls below your stop price. Sticking to a trading plan can be hard, so consider implementing automatic stop orders to prevent decisions that could be impacted by emotions and cause an ultimately catastrophic loss. Learning to walk away is the hardest and most important lesson day traders need to learn.

Cutting Your Losses

It's important that you weigh your trades fairly equally so that one bad trade doesn't undo all of the profits earned by your other winners. This risk management strategy is called balancing risk. By utilizing small increments to adjust risk, no one stock will have the power to destroy your overall performance. Never assume that one winning stock can save you from a losing stock. Day trading is high risk, but that doesn't mean you should make your stocks unnecessarily high risk. Remember that most trades that are truly strong will prove their worth almost immediately.

While day trading can be a gamble, using data, understanding the potential risks of each trade, and following your risk management rules will provide you with a successful trading plan. Do not be reckless or irrational with your judgments; this will hinder your performance and possibly even destroy your career. Set an entry price for day trades and do not add to stocks that are below that rate. When a trade is failing, cut your losses and refocus on a new opportunity.

On the other hand, it is important to note that the potential for big winners increases by adding to winning trades. Remember, the goal is to cap your losses and grow your winners as efficiently as possible. A good profit loss ratio means that you can trade with profit despite an accuracy rate of 50%. The next chapter will discuss how to pick the best stocks, but without risk management, those stocks could become worthless. Combining your trading techniques with risk management strategies will deliver you success as a day trader.

CHAPTER 3: STOCK SELECTION

When combined with the risk management and emotional conditioning strategies we discussed in the previous two chapters, stock selection can dramatically improve your opportunities for success as a day trader. It is important that you do not become overwhelmed by the wide range of stocks available and select stocks that are profitable specifically for day trading. There are certain qualities that make some stocks better for day trading, even if they wouldn't catch the attention of a long-term investment trader.

Finding Your Stocks for Day Trading

Because most day traders trade so many different stocks over the course of a short period of time, it's important to select stocks with heavy trading volume and volatility. Stocks trading at extreme highs or lows can drive high levels of retail interest and, consequently, heavy volume. Day traders should follow these patterns and trade stocks on days when there is a gap between periods of high relative volume.

Note that, like anything, gaps should still be scrutinized. For example, buy outs can cause a stock to change in price and increase in volume. However, remember that the value will remain fixed all day, so gaps caused by buyouts should be disregarded by day traders.

A good practice is to follow the stocks that other people are trading and focus on trading those same stocks. Day traders should seek stocks that are trading on above average volume and ignore chart patterns that seem to indicate a good buying opportunity because they are controlled by high-frequency trading computers. Following daily volume or using stock scanning software can help day traders find the "right" stocks. Researching the catalysts to establish reasons for why a particular stock is moving up or down is also very useful.

It is crucial that you make the chart patterns one of your top considerations when evaluating a stock. News regarding a stock can pray upon our emotions and cause panicked judgments about buying or selling stocks. While news released from direct sources such as the company, its competition, its shareholders, or a reputable analyst firm or agency should be heeded, other sources should be scrutinized heavily.

Stocks to Watch

There are other qualities of stocks that are important for day traders to follow. For instance, stocks that make huge intraday moves (more than 100%) are known as former runners and have the opportunity to deliver big profits to day traders. Their characteristics will be that of a good stock with low float and strong breaking news.

Float is a stock's available outstanding shares on the open market. The number of shares set in the initial public offering becomes the float. The buyback program can cause a decrease in float and share price while selling more shares on the open market can cause an increase. However, the value of the shares decreases as more shares are sold.

A low float and solid catalyst can contribute to 100% intraday moves for day traders, but a large float will not likely deliver a large profit. Therefore, the float should be one of the first qualities you evaluate when considering a stock. Note that float rotations occur when the entire float of available shares is traded. Day traders should be less interested in stocks with a float of more than 500 million shares as they will be less volatile.

Monitoring Stocks

It is useful to monitor the high and low of the stock on the previous day and trade during a fresh breakout. Stocks that have been particularly active on one trading day may carry that energy over into the next day; these are called follow through days. Inside days occur when trading happens inside the high and low of the previous day and often follow volatile days. The lack of momentum or price action that occurs on these days makes them less opportune times to trade a stock.

As you might expect, risk can be greatly reduced by trading the right stocks at the right time. Day traders need to focus on highly active stocks and be ready to act quickly (and smartly) in response to changing markets. Volatility is an essential market component for day traders, but it does require careful, calculated observation and action.

For example, breaking news can cause the strength of a stock to alter dramatically, leading to a volatility halt. This phenomenon is called an intraday extreme, and it presents an opportunity for day traders if the stock was trading on high relative volume, even without an obvious catalyst.

Now that you understand some of the fundamentals of finding and monitoring potential trade opportunities, the next chapter will go into further detail on how to use and read charts to find more complex opportunities that will improve your performance as a day trader.

CHAPTER 4: READING CANDLESTICKS

Although intraday stock charts, as mentioned in the previous chapter, are an important indicator to follow, day traders must remember that each stock is traded in the framework of its daily chart. By providing a visual price history of a particular stock, these charts provide context for current stock prices. This chapter will help you set up basic stock charts and teach you how to follow patterns such as support and resistance levels.

Candlestick charts

Day traders typically use candlestick charts because they can show any time frame of trading that you desire. Daily charts, 60-minute charts, 15-minute charts, 5-minute charts, and 1-minute charts are the most commonly used candlestick charts. These charts provide information regarding the high, low, open, and close of the period. The real body is the center of the candle and the lines that lead to the high and the low are the upper and lower candle wicks, or "shadows."

Decoding Candlestick Shapes

The shape of the candle provides information about the market sentiment, and multiple candlesticks can reveal further chart patterns.

When the open price and the close price are very similar, a very small candle body, called a doji candlestick, is formed. This indicates a buyer-seller standoff and indecision in the market. Potential reversals can be indicated by the tails of the candle. Topping and bottoming tails occur when long upper or lower wicks appear on candles at the tops or bottoms of long trends.

Candles with small bodies and lower wicks that are long and larger than the bodies are called hammer candles. When hammer candles occur in the context of a long downtrend, they can indicate a selloff where prices were quickly pushed back up by buyers. When the next candle breaks the high of the hammer, a candle over candle confirmation occurs and signals a reversal.

Inverted hammers that occur at the end of a long uptrend have a long topping tail, indicating a quickly reversed surge of buying, and a small real body. This pattern indicates that a battle between buyers and sellers in which the sellers came out on top.

Long body candles that are green and continuously surge upon opening are indicative of a bullish market and close at the high. Day traders want to avoid buying after a long body candle and aim to be holding while a long body candle is forming.

An extreme bearish sentiment is indicated by a red long body candle that opens and sells off for the entire period. A reversal pattern of three red long body candles in a row, ending with a bottoming tail candle, indicates a reversal pattern that day traders should be hunting for. A candle over candle entry on the first candle to make a new high following a selloff is a good strategy if the bottoming tail also coincides with a daily support level.

CHAPTER 5: USING CANDLESTICKS

Now that you understand how to read candlesticks on your charts, this chapter will focus on teaching you how to utilize your charts in a way that will bring you success as a day trader.

Note that keeping charts simple and clean avoids unneeded complexity and confusion. Of the thousands of downloadable technical indicators, most are lagging indicators that are unnecessary additions to your trading plan. Although technical indicators attempt to place a current price action in a context that could predict future price action, a reversal is usually already in progress by the time the technical indicator can predict and confirm it.

The best traders know how to anticipate moves by evaluating candlestick charts. Like the Holy Grail syndrome, trying to "hunt" for the prefect indicators can keep you from success. This chapter will teach you how to effectively use technical indicators to improve your performance.

Which Should I Look For?

Monitoring the 1 minute, 5, minute, and daily charts will show the price action for the day as well as the past 3-6 months. Windows and triggers can be identified by drawing horizontal line trends on the daily chart. Support and resistance lines on the 1 min and 5 min chart can help you determine how much room for a profit a certain trade might have. Still, keep in mind that the simpler you keep your charts, the better.

Day traders should pay attention to moving averages in particular. Moving averages will show you both the intraday and daily levels of support and resistance for most stocks. The average price of a stock over a set period of time will give you the moving averages. Stocks trading above or below their moving averages indicate uptrends and downtrends respectively.

The average price over a set number of periods will give you the simple moving average. The exponential moving action is calculated by taking the average over the set number of period. However, exponential moving averages put most weight on the recent price action, causing the moving action to respond quickly to recent moves.

Therefore, most day traders should focus on exponential moving action and include the 9 EMA, 20 EMA, 50 EMA and 200 EMA on their charts. Stocks trading along the 9 EMA indicate strength. To reduce risk, day traders should buy trending stocks close to moving average support. Reversal trades should be made when the price is moving a way from the 9 EMA and extremely extended. The 200 EMA on the 5 minute and daily carts can reveal support or resistance, but day traders should be cautious because it is possible for stocks to consolidate at one level before breaking away.

The Volume Weighed Average Price can be used by day traders to reveal the average daily price of a sock while factoring how many shares were traded. Stocks that are extended away from their equilibrium point indicate a countertrend set up. Trend based trading requires that you pay attention to entries with close proximity to the VWAP.

Simple volume bars indicate the number of shares of volume traded over the course of a candlestick period. They provide signals regarding the increasing and decreasing volume and momentum that can direct a day trader that a trend is shifting in direction.

Extreme Trading

When timing reversal trade at extremes, using Bollinger Bands on your 5-minute charts can be particularly useful. To find the default indicator setting, use a 2.0 standard deviation Bollinger Band and a 20 period moving average. Day traders engaging in counter trading should avoid entering a reversal trade too early.

A relative strength index, which represents the strength of a stock, below 20 or above 80 signals and intraday extreme, similar to a candle outside the Bollinger Bands. However, the RSI on its own is not a reliable signal to buy or sell because it can linger at extremes for extended periods of time. Therefore, it is only useful to include the RSI on your chart when you include a filter that only displays stock ideas when an RSI is below 20 or above 80.

CHAPTER 6: DAILY CHART PATTERNS

This chapter continues the discussion of charts and chart patterns, focusing on daily chart patterns in particular. While one day of price action can be represented by a candlestick on the daily charts, day traders should focus primarily on the patterns demonstrated on the 1-minute and 5-minute charts. Daily support and resistance levels should also be identified and monitored. These factors will contribute to the technical analysis and help reveal technical break out patterns.

There factors can cause a stock to thrive and make unanticipated strong intraday moves despite poor performance on your daily charts. This is because it is possible for a strong enough catalyst to supersede daily resistance levels.

Events like these remind us that the behavior of a stock does not always follow what we've determined from a fundamental analysis. Therefore, it is essential that day traders pay attention to chart patterns, understand levels, and be prepared for the impact particularly strong or week catalysts can have on your daily chart.

Understanding Support and Resistance

A support level occurs when a stock continuously hits a price on a downside without being able to break that price. A resistance level is determined when the same event occurs to the upside. Every time the stock reaches the price level but fails to break it, the support or resistance level gains validity.

False breakouts can occur when a level briefly breaks, and prices reverse. Day traders can fall victim to false breakouts if they take a position before receiving confirmation of a breakout. However, day traders can avoid these situations by learning how to read signs of breakouts as well as false breakouts. This skill, in conjunction with knowledge of support and resistance levels, can help day traders determine biases for stocks on their morning watch list and identify setups and trade potential.

For example, areas of support and resistance can be identified every morning when reviewing stocks trading on above-average volume on your daily chart. A lack of resistance on a chart can signal increased potential, provided the catalyst is strong.

Ascending and descending support and resistance lines, though not as obvious, can be used in addition to horizontal and support resistance lines. These lines typically are marked based on large trends over a period of months and occur less often than horizontal lines.

Using Windows and Triggers

Daily charts can reveal a potential for break out when a price action enters a window with no support or resistance; stocks with breakout potential are the stocks you want to trade. However, you should note that high relative volume (often due to a catalyst) is necessary is required to get a big move. Therefore, you should only monitor stocks that are in play as a result of current events or news.

Potential resistance levels with a window of no resistance larger than the Average True Range (ATR) of a stock are called triggers. Big windows, created by long body candles or gaps, with big triggers at the top and bottom should be of particular interest to day traders.

Filling in the Gaps

Gaps occur when a stock opens significantly higher or lower than it did on the previous day of trading as a result of a fundamental catalyst. The large windows formed by gaps are filled when a stock's price enters the gap window on a chart. The lack of resistance inside a window causes the gap to be filled rapidly. Until the price can close it, the window will stay open and legitimate.

Windows created by gaps typically receive more buying attention than windows created by body candles because they are more obvious in appearance. Experienced traders will be able to identify complex patterns, meaning there will be less volume at spots of critical breakout in these situations. Therefore, day traders should focus on the simpler patterns where more opportunities are present.

The Whole and Half of It

Support and resistance also appear as stocks advance towards whole and half dollars. These marks can be useful for setting stops and strengthening setups for stocks of all price ranges. However, if you are going to engage in trading over or under whole and half dollars, be sure to only do so with stocks trading in intraday extremes or on high relative volume.

Gapping-up The Works

Gapped-up stocks will often open around moving average resistance and, without a strong catalyst, contend with the daily resistance levels. Stocks gapping up or down will break up and away or down and away, respectively, from their moving averages. Using our charts to identify daily windows and gaps, positions of moving averages, and levels of trend line support will help build a day trader's bias against a stock.

As a form of support or resistance, moving averages on an intraday level can be very useful as entry opportunities for day traders.

CHAPTER 7: BROKERS AND ORDERS

This chapter will elaborate upon the process of buying and selling stocks and discuss how to choose a broker that is best for you.

Comparing Brokers

Fast executions and competitive commissions are the two crucial qualities day traders should look for in their brokers. Day traders do not benefit from full-service brokers because their services are geared towards part-time investors interested in retirement account management and less positions.

Day traders would suffer because of the lag time of the slower platforms offered by this type of broker. Active day traders require quick, top-notch execution speed and benefit from the ability to choose which electronic communication network they wish to use to send orders; this is called direct access routing.

Note that brokers offering commissions of $4.95 or less per each trade and direct access routing are best suited for day traders.

May I Take Your Order?

As a day trader, you'll need to be familiar with market orders, limit orders, and stop orders.

A market order can be placed by providing your broker with the number of shares of a particular stock that you wish to buy. When the order is processed, the current market price is applied to the shares. Because no specific price is stipulated beforehand, this can be a particularly risky order in a volatile market.

Limit orders are similar to market orders, except you can stipulate the maximum price you are willing to spend. When the order is sent, you will receive the maximum number of shares within the maximum price you set, as long as the price of the stock does not change too rapidly.

Stop orders are used to sell a certain number of shares at a trigger price. The stop order will not be executed until the trigger price is hit, at which time the order will automatically be sent. Day traders can use stop orders to initiate new positions or exit long and short positions. Buy stops are particularly useful for taking advantage of breakouts.

Market Depth (Level2) Windows

Once a relationship with a broker has been established, you will want to view several different windows from the platform, including a Market Depth (Level2) window, a Time and Sales window, and an Order Entry window.

The Market Depth window shows Level1 prices, or the National Best Bid and Best Offer, on top. However, day traders are really only concerned with the Market Depth, or Level2. The Level2 provide a greater depth of information by showing the number of buyers and sellers along with the bid and the ask. This can give us a visual indication of the market sentiment and help us decide if it's a good time to make a trade.

Lining up the price support and resistance on the Level2 with the support and resistance on the chart is an indicator of value. However, it is possible to manipulate the market, and day traders should be on the look out for spoofing.

Get Your Timing Right

Because orders and prices are always changing the Level2, it can be difficult to learn how to efficiently use it. This is where execution speed, ECN, and general efficiency become essential for your success as a day trader. Utilizing a time and sales window, for example, will help you follow transactions as they go through.

Your time is limited when preparing to make a trade so it's important to make use of your pre-market time to get orders ready before the market opens. Once you begin trading, hot keys will assist you with high-speed management of your positions.

Hot keys can be used for entering and exiting trades, as well as placing stop orders and canceling orders and are particularly useful at the open of the trading day when the market trades on highest volume. By eliminating delays caused by manual entry, you can avoid some of the losses that are incurred by slow action.

Below is a list of hot keys that you should memorize:

Control + X (Sell half position on bid price)

Control + L (Sell half position on ask price)

Control + Z (Sell full position on bid)

Control + B (Set stop at average cost or breakeven)

Control + 1 (Set stop loss for full position -11 cents)

Control + 2 (Set stop loss for full position -21 cents)

Control + 3 (Set stop loss for full position -31 cents)

Be sure that your confirmation windows remain on while you are still learning your hot keys so you do not make a technical error that ruins a trade.

CHAPTER 8: BUILDING MOMENTUM

The next step in building your day trading skills is to learn how to find your entry using chart patterns and setups. Chart setups provide you with opportunities to safely enter stocks that have demonstrated their strength. Although patterns may seem obscure at first, with more experience, these setups will become obvious and useful for finding breakout spots.

Remember that to take full advantage of momentum trading, you'll need to buy near moving average support or look for the bottom of bull flag pullbacks, keeping your risk low and your potential for reward high. You'll want to keep an eye out for flags and pullbacks that occur while the formation of a chart pattern is still in progress.

As we've discussed before, all trades should only be made with justified risk. Patterns can provide a max loss price through their well-defined support levels that you can base your position size on. Make sue that your profit target represents twice your risk so you have the crucial 2:1 profit loss we discussed in previous chapters.

Keep in mind that the patterns discussed in this chapter only apply to stocks that are strong enough to be worthy of trading. Day traders may find themselves seizing upon stocks that have already made large intraday moves, while investors might pass on these opportunities; this is because day traders can use the intraday support levels to manage their risk and see the trend through for another 5 to 10%.

Limit orders should always be used to enter and exit positions. However, as a day trader, you may find yourself adjusting your stop loss to breakeven more than you might expect; this is so you have the opportunity to cap your losses but also ride out stocks that have the potential to become big winners.

Momentum Stocks and Setups

Keeping in mind that momentum can be traded both long and short, the momentum strategy setups that you will want to become familiar with include Parabolic Movers, Moving Average Pullbacks, Flat Bottom Breakdowns, Flat Top Breakouts, Bear Flags, and Bull flags.

You should note momentum stocks with a low float below 10 million shares, as their supply available to trade is very limited. The float will help you determine the trade's potential and justify the risk.

Keep an eye out for surging stocks before the market opens and continue to monitor momentum stock scanners throughout the day; this is a great way to identify potential opportunities.

Pullbacks

When you see a momentum stock making a fresh breakout, you should prepare to potentially trade the first and second pullback as well as the breakout. A bull flag, a flat top breakout, or a moving average retracement are some of the forms these pullbacks may take. Pullbacks will appear on the 5- and 1-minute charts.

Stocks respond positively to the first and second pullbacks because there is demand from traders who missed the first breakout and subsequent pullback if the stock is demonstrating strength. Most entries become riskier after the second pullback, except in cases of consolidation periods. Therefore, smaller position sizes should be used if you intend to enter after the second pullback before a long period of consolidation and another fresh breakout.

Breakouts

A flat top breakout is a bullish pattern that gives clear indications of breakout spots. This pattern appears best on the 5-minute chart and indicates stocks that have moved up at least 4% within a few hours without pulling back or selling off. You should keep an eye out for consolidating flat top breakouts that occur below whole and half dollar levels where stocks would typically find resistance.

Look for an ascending support level and set your stop just below that trend line when you enter a flat top breakout pattern. An instantaneous volume surge will occur as soon as the price breaks above the resistance point. Provided that the level holds, a continued rally should occur indicating that prior resistance has become support.

Monitor your daily chart for nearby triggers and windows when you see a breakout setup forming. You will want to use your Level2 to identify the apex point for your moment to buy; this is the breakout price. When you buy a flat top break out, you are purchasing a stock at its high of the day, which is risky. Start with half size and set your stop at the ascending support line at the wedge's bottom in case the stock fails to break out or drops below breakout price. You can add to your position once you are confident in the breakout.

Breakdowns

Flat bottom breakdowns provide the same opportunities as the flat top breakout. Weak stocks that consolidate just above critical support levels present a low-risk entry with the potential for quick profit. Identify catalysts and use your daily chart to confirm you have a 2:1 profit loss ratio.

Bull Flags

Bull flag breakouts, unlike flat top breakouts, indicate a slight pullback following the initial strong move. They are traded best on the 1- and 5-minute charts and will be signaled by a move of somewhere between 3 and 5 long body green candles followed by a pull back and 1 to 3 smaller red candles. You'll want to keep an eye out for surging stocks with high relative volume; when they pullback 25% of the move at most, they can form bull flag opportunities.

Remember that purchases during a bull flag should be made when the first candle reaches a new high, giving the momentum back to the bulls. Do not confuse bull flags with flat top breakouts—bull flags should not be entered at the height of day. Look for the initial move up to have strong volume and the pullback to coincide with low volume. As the stock returns to the highs, you should see high volume. High volume on the pullback is a sign that the stock might reverse rather that move higher.

Bear Flags

A strong sell off with a light volume, followed by a new low set by the first candle in a round of selling indicates a bear flag. Flags will typically appear on a 1-minute chart as a result of rapid price drop. To find the greatest bear flags, you should be looking for stocks showing a surge of volume. The prices of stocks forming bear flags on lighter volumes are influenced by the strength of the overall market, so you will want to select very obvious setups when shorting stocks.

Flag Patterns and Moving Average Retracements

A stock stops being a bull flag or flat top breakout pattern when it rapidly moves up, then pulls back between three and five candles and consolidates; this situation indicates a flag pattern. Flag patterns are of use to day traders on the 5-minute chart if the stock consolidates at least above the 9 EMA support; prices that hold above this level indicate a strong trend.

The opportunity for low-risk entry for these stocks presents itself when the 9 EMA undergoes a pullback. When you see an opportunity to use this setup, adjusting your stop to breakeven and selling half through the high of day spike is the best plan; when you see an exit indicator, you can deal with the remaining position.

If you are trying to trade conservatively, you want to enter most trades when they are close to moving average support, and when the moving average is broken by price action. Waiting until the price breaks below the 9 EMA is promising because it gives you the opportunity to avoid trading at high speed.

Moving average retracements can also show opportunities in weak stocks; simply follow the same rules on the 0 EAM pop that you would use for shorting weak stocks on the 9 EMA pullback trade.

Buying a Higher High

When you find a stock with a history of long bias on the daily chart, there is the possibility for a pullback entry. If the 1-minute chart and 5-minute chart show entry signals near the same price, you have an apex point for a pattern to break out or down.

The Ups and Downs of Parabolic Moves

A stock that moves straight up or down undergoes what is known as a parabolic move. This pattern is great for day traders because it signals an irrationally strong or weak stock with a strong catalyst and daily chart.

To trade a parabolic stock, you should monitor your 1-minute chart for situations that feature a short pullback due to a bull flag or flat top breakout. Once you make an entry, sell half of your position, adjust your stop, and hold on! Parabolic movers are risky stocks, so you'll need to use smaller positions in the early stages.

Alternatively, you can try to guess how high or how low the parabolic move will go, but this is a very risky—and occasionally rewarding—plan. You should only enter reversal trades with a quarter of your planned position size, so your success is not dependent upon picking the exact reversal point. You can choose to add once the reversal is confirmed.

Regardless of which plan you are using, remember to continue to consider risk management when trading parabolic stocks. Keep your emotions in check, as the risks are particularly high in these types of trades.

Gap and Go

The Gap and Go momentum strategy seizes upon a pattern for stocks showing strength before the market opens, followed by a surge after the market opens. These stocks will typically have high relative volume throughout the day. Utilizing the pre-market charts to gauge strength enables you to capitalize on volatility that might scare other trades away early in the day. Note that this strategy should be used on stocks valued at $20 or under.

Stocks that have the biggest percentage gaps are your best Gap and Go candidates. Before taking the trade, confirm that the stock is being moved by a catalyst and that it is consolidating close to its pre-market range. Analyze technically and fundamentally when researching a catalyst and use reliable, confirmed new sources

When you are sure of the catalyst you can start mapping the triggers and windows on your daily chart and determining your entry and stop prices. Unless the stock has 500K or more in pre-market volume, you should wait to trade when the market is open. Include two to four Gap and Go candidates with the most obvious set ups on your watch list and mark the pre-market highs and lows before the markets open.

If your pre-market chart shows a bull flag or flat top breakout, trade according to the pattern. Look for a heavy offer on the Level2 at the opening of the market to confirm resistance at the apex point. Attempt to place your order moments before the break so you are sure the apex point will be broken. Protect the winner by taking profit on the first surge and then adjusting your stop to breakeven.

Use the first 1-minute candle as your trigger when a Gap and Go candidate opens in the middle of support and resistance levels; the top will be our entry price and the low is your stop. If the high of the first 1-minute candle is broken by the second 1-minute candle, you are seeing an opening range breakout (ORB) and you should buy. If an ORB does not occur within twenty minutes, you should start following another stock from your watch list. Remember that the best Gap and Go stocks will often offer several opportunities.

If you miss a pre-market flag breakout or ORB, your next opportunity to enter will be the first pullback. This is a very conservative technique for trading Gap and Go stocks and beginner traders may benefit from using this strategy to start. However, make sure that you look for a flat top breakout, 9 EMA, or traditional bull flag when you see the first pullback.

Some Gap and Go stocks will only allow you to use a Red to Green move as a setup. This set up occurs if the stock price falls below the open price before surging above the open price again, causing the stock to change from red to green within the day. Because this causes shorts that add buying value while long-biased traders enter, there is the potential for a big breakout to occur.

Be aware that by entering this setup you are dealing with weaker stocks that have the potential to be overpowered by sellers. If you are going to make a trade with this setup, you should use the 1- or 5-minute chart to enter when the first candle makes a new high after a washout.

Plan to sell half your position when you make what was risked and adjust your stop to breakeven. If the move is strong, you will trade the first pullback that follows the breakout. However, if the setup returns to red within the day, it's time to exit, even if it's for a loss.

Entry Requirements

Look for the following qualities before you enter a momentum or Gap and Go setup:

1. 100k in volume within the first minute of the market opening.

2. For Momentum Trading Strategy trades, volume should be at 1 million.

3. A 2:1 profit loss ration can be achieved.

4. The high relative volume of the stock is 2 or more

5. A clear, obvious pattern.

6. The 9 EMA or 20 EMA support levels are close to the entry point.

7. Float is 50 million shares or less. VWAP trading strategies are the exception.

8. Strong catalyst

9. Clean daily chart featuring windows and triggers.

Preparing Your Entry

Use the Level2 to find tight spreads below five cents; these stocks will be the most easy to manage. You will want to make momentum trades based upon a high relative volume on your 1-minute chart. Keep in mind the price that you plan to buy at and look for it at the top of the one minute candle or apex of the pattern.

For momentum setups, you should enter with a half sized position and expect immediate resolution. Therefore, if immediate resolution does not occur, you should exit or reduce your position size. You can also double later if adjusting your stop to breakeven is possible.

Take larger positions when trading with 5-minute chart patterns. Like the 1-minute entry, you will buy the top of the flat top breakout, the bull flag breaking point, or the pattern apex. Look for patterns of momentum trades of strong stock during the midday when using the 5-minute chart. When you do enter, your stop should be set at the low of the pullback, close but under the 9 EMA, or under the ascending support line.

Setting Profit Targets

To estimate your profit target on a momentum trade, you should identify technical areas of resistance on your daily chart. If a momentum trade approaches a logical resistance point, you should attempt to take profit, then adjust your stop to breakeven or move it into the profit zone while maintaining a partial position. However, do not hold stocks that are up 20-30% intraday overnight.

Knowing When to Exit

There are three important signs to exit that you should keep an eye out for when trading momentum:

1. A 5-minute candle reaches a new low before you have the opportunity to scale out half of your position.

2. The 5-minute chart shows price breaking below the 9 EMA. This is an indicator to exit even if you have scaled out. Momentum stock with strength trend up the 9 EMA before consolidating down at the moving average. You can hold on to a partial position and continue to gauge the strength of the trend until it breaks below the 9 EMA.

3. You get stopped out after adjusting your stop to breakeven. Remember to base your stop price on a specific support level or you maximum loss. Adjust your stops to breakeven and, eventually, into the profit zone, as the trade progresses. This gives you the opportunity to trade the full range until your stop fires.

As always, you want to follow these indicators by exiting and moving on to another opportunity, capping your losses and increasing your chances to find a winner.

Chapter 9: Trading In Reverse

When a big move occurs, and you fail to take advantage of it, know that there is still another opportunity to make a trade. While it is difficult to make predictions about big moves to the upside or downside, we know that such moves will ultimately produce a reversal.

Reversal trading provides you with the opportunity to buy a stock when it is weak, giving you a fantastic profit loss ratio that gives you room for a lower accuracy rate while still profiting.

To take advantage of countertrending strategies, you'll need to understand how to identify stocks that are likely to make big bounces. Because they behave similar to a rubber band that is stretched and then snaps back with great power, extended stocks are the ones we want to keep our eyes on.

Using Candlesticks When Trading Reversals

If you are trading reversals, your setups should have somewhere between 3 and 10 consecutive long body candles at the high or low of the day; the more consecutive long body candles, the better. Look for the first candle to be positioned outside the Bollinger bands, indicating an extreme move.

Because it is challenging to properly time reversals, you'll want to check a few additional indicators, such as looking at the Relative Strength Index to confirm that the stock is either above 80 or below 20.

The reversal bar is the final candle, and it should be in the form of a doji, a hammer or inverted hammer, or a topping or bottoming tail outside the Bollinger bands. Your stop and entry price will be based upon the high and the low of this candle, respectively.

Finding Your Reversal Setup

You daily chart will help you confirm which reversal setups are the best. Look for the reversal point to running into a moving average or touching critical areas of support or resistance. You should also monitor the volume; if the last candle shows the highest volume of the day, you should consider making a reversal trade.

Although many stocks that technically meet the requirements for a reversal will show up on your reversal scanner, you should be very careful about which reversal trades you take. Be particularly cautious when on days when a whole sector is showing signs of weakness and look for the following ten requirements when considering reversal trades:

1. Three or more consecutive 5-minute candles

2. Candles are on or outside the Bollinger bands

3. Stock has reached high or low of day

4. RSI is greater than 80 or less than 20

5. Check float, as usual

6. Final candle meets characteristics of a reversal candle

7. Daily resistance can be bounced off of

8. Entry is supported by the overall market

9. A 2:1 profit loss ratio can be reasonably achieved

10. The 5-minute chart shows at least 30 cents to the 9 EMA

Once you have found a stock that fits the description above, take a quarter or half size position with a 20 cent stop or a stop when it reaches its high or low of the day. Exit when the stock breaks a new high or low.

Entering and Exiting

Base your first attempt to enter a reversal trade on the 1-minute chart and then confirm with the 5-minute chart. These low-risk entries will provide you with the chance to bail out if necessary. It's also worth noting that buying the first pullback of reversals after confirmation is one of the safest strategies you can use.

Remember to adjust your stop to break even or a 10 cent loss when you choose to double your position. If the price touches the 9 EMA on the five minute chart or you reach your 2:1 profit loss ratio, sell half and adjust your stop to breakeven. If the price goes beyond the 9 EMA, adjust your stop to the other side of the 9 EMA. Complete another partial sell at the VWAP and so you still have a small position to move back over the VWAP and to make a possible swing trade.

The appearance of a candle over candle pattern on the 5-minute chart is a strong confirmation of a reversal. When using the 5-minute chart to make your entry, use the top of a candle outside the Bollinger bands as your entry or double up point and the bottom of that same candle as your stop. Take the trade if there is 30 cents of profit potential to the 9 EMA. Continue to monitor the 1-minute chart as well.

Do not try to change a reversal setup to a momentum step up as they will very rarely work interchangeably. If a reversal is not working, simply keep an eye out for a better opportunity instead of putting yourself at risk for a snapback.

CHAPTER 10: USING SCANNERS TO BUILD A WATCH LIST

Finding the right stock scanner will make finding your trade setups that much easier. Your scanner should provide you with setups in real-time, so you have the best opportunities to profit off of them. Stock scanners enable you to see only the specific types of stock or chart patterns that you wish to see, enabling your selection process to be as clear as possible. Alternatively, you can use your scanner to search in broad terms as well.

By choosing your trading tools carefully, you can relieve yourself of some of the complexities and challenges of day trading. Some scanners will show you the historical data of a stock scan, enabling you to see alerts from previous days or weeks instantly.

Even if you have many scanners that you use, you should try to sort them into momentum opportunities and reversal opportunities, as these are the stocks that will provide you with the highest percentage of successful trades, if used correctly.

Scanning for Gaps

Add checking your gap scanner to your morning routine so you can identify stocks with the largest percentages of gap as well as the largest volume. Pre-market volume is a good indicator of what to watch in the day ahead.

By the time the market opens you should have a list of 4 to 6 stocks that demonstrate potential for a 5 to 10 percent intraday move. These are the stocks you will watch the closest all day, as you will be expecting to see certain patterns before they come.

Building and Using Your Watch List

You will build a watch list every morning and follow them throughout your day of trading. Remember that this does not mean that the stocks on your watch list will be the stocks that move the most, however.

For momentum stocks, you will want to set a filter on your scanner that identifies stocks in high relative volume and 15-minute volume surge. Because the watch list is based on pre-market volume and breaking news can occur over the course of the trading day, you will need to be able to quickly analyze stocks that are not on your watch list when they come into play. Remember to always confirm catalysts before you act on them.

When you are using a stock scanner to identify reversal trades, use the filters to set a minimum volume of 500,000 shares, priced at $15 to $250, and at least 4 consecutive candles. Once you see your results, further sort them by searching for RSI position within Bollinger bands and percentage of daily change. Whatever stocks remain will be the stocks you will want to consider for a reversal trade that day.

CHAPTER 11: 3 STEPS TO SUCCESS

This final chapter will discuss how to set up a trading plan with realistic expectations, setting a foundation for steady growth and eventual success as a day trader. Your profits might be small or non-existent at first, but your goal should be to start small, survive, grow, and THEN thrive. Rushing your growth by skipping steps or ignoring rules and strategies you've learned in this text will likely lead to mistakes that can jeopardize your career as a day trader.

The three step trading plan that follows will incorporate the lessons covered throughout this book to help you get started on the path to success in day trading.

Getting Started

Your first 3 months will begin the same way every day, Monday through Friday. After waking up, you should engage in 30 minutes of aerobic exercise to practice emotional and mental conditioning. Between your workout and 9:15 AM, you should check in with gap scan and create watch list of 4-6 stocks, including the news catalysts, entry prices, and stop prices for each stock. By 9:30 AM, you should prepare an order for four of the top "Gap and Go" candidates using your order entry window and following the rules of the Gap and Go Trading Strategy.

At the opening of the market, press the buy button and begin managing your open positions. Throughout the day, continue to look for trade opportunities on the Momentum scanners and the Reversal scanners.

Note that this trading plan requires you to take about 10 trades a day to practice the experience of managing a trade using your strategies. Every trade should be tracked in your spreadsheet so you can review which strategies work best for you. Once you've mastered one strategy, you can move on to becoming proficient in another.

Month 1—Step 1 (Simulated Account)

The goal of your first month is to trade at a 50% success rate in a simulated environment. $50 can be risked per trade, and your max position size should not exceed 100 shares on stocks above $20 and 200 shares on stocks below $20.

Because your daily max loss should be no more than $150, you may find yourself shutting down the platform early in the day, which is an important lesson in risk management that you will want to carry with you to the live account.

Remember that success in Month 1 will not be defined by total profits; rather, your focus should be on your profit loss ratio and percentage of success. If you achieve a good profit loss ratio, you can proceed on to Month 2. Otherwise, it is in your best interest to complete another month of simulated trading so you can gain additional experience.

Month 2 – Step 2 (Live Account)

Using what you learned in Month 1 and the data you gathered, begin Month 2 by examining and adjusting your strategy. Once you feel confident enough, switch to a live trading account and begin trading with the same restrictions you followed in Month 1. After one month of successful live trading, move on to Month 3.

Month 3 – Step 2

You will begin Month 3 by increasing the amount you risk to $100 per trade. Your max position will increase to 200 shares and 400 shares for stocks over and under $20, respectively. Set a daily profit target at $300 and a max daily loss at $300. Your weekly goal will be $900, three times your daily goal. This month will require you to practice the skills you learned in the first two months but with higher stakes.

Month 4 –Step 3

Your final month will have a max position of 500 shares for stocks exceeding $20 and 1000 shares for stocks below $20. Your risk per trade will increase to $200, and your goal will be to reach a daily profit target of $600 a day and a weekly target of $1800 total. After completing this step successfully, an annual profit of $100,000 comes into reach.

You may find that you need to repeat some of these steps several times before you are ready to move on, and that is ok; learning how and when to make adjustments will contribute to your overall success as a day trader. Remember to persevere and maintain discipline—the risk management strategies and other techniques you've been practice will keep you moving forward on the road to success!

CONCLUSION

The challenges of day trading are hard to master, and the chances of building a successful career are only 1 in 10. However, as this book has discussed, this reality does not have to mean failure is inevitable.

Day trading can be a lucrative, exciting way to invest and trade when practiced correctly. We've identified some of the areas where both novice and experienced traders go wrong and gone into detail about how to avoid these situations. Despite volatility and other risks that you will encounter as a day trader, the lessons from this book will help you to respond to these challenges. Do not become discouraged by minor mistakes; take those mistakes and apply your knowledge from this book to identify what caused you to fail and how you should have managed trade in hindsight.

The risk management techniques discussed in this book will help you to further discipline your thinking and provide you with a long, successful career as a day trader. The more you practice these skills, the easier it will become to apply them quickly and accurately during your trades. Remember the rules you set for yourself about profits, losses, and chart management.

Equipped with the lessons from this text, you should now feel ready to take on the world of day trading with confidence and awareness. Good Luck!

Book Description

Day trading is a risky Endeavour that typically produces more tales of failure than success. However, before you give up on day trading, it's essential that you recognize the mistakes that cause so many day traders to fail. In addition to choosing the wrong stocks traders who fail to manage risk, are unable to find proper entries, and do not recognize the importance of following the rules that go with proven strategies, will continue to lose in the market without understanding why.

This book will introduce you to the fundamentals of predicting volatility and risk management. Using the strategies and tips for selling and buying, you will learn to minimize your risk and maximize your profit.

This guide will act as your roadmap for getting back on the pathway to successful daytrading.

Thank you for reading. If you could spare a minute and leave this book a positive Amazon review. It really helps! Thanks again

Want more? Checkout my author page and see what other books you might be interested in!

- John

Printed in Great Britain
by Amazon